Traditional
Cornish Recipes

Carolyn Martin

Bossiney Books · Exeter

Acknowledgements

The curators of some of the stately homes in Cornwall have been most courteous in answering my queries. In particular, I would like to thank Samantha Goodrich at Trerice for allowing me to use her recipe for lemon meringue pie. Also, I am grateful for the help given by the staff at Kresen Kernow and the Cornwall library service. Finally, I must thank my husband for his patience in reading through my manuscript, correcting mistakes and his enthusiastic appetite for sampling some of the more unusual recipes – usually with a good helping of clotted cream.

First published 2022 by
Bossiney Books Ltd, 68 Thorndale Courts, Whitycombe Way,
Exeter, EX4 2NY

www.bossineybooks.com

ISBN 978-1-906474-92-8

Cover design by Beth Paisley

Printed in Great Britain by Booths Print, Penryn

Contents

A note on the recipes

Unless otherwise stated, most recipes in this collection are for four people. Imperial and metric measurements and weights are given and, as fresh yeast is difficult to purchase, the dried yeast equivalent is given. If using fast action dried yeast, this can be added directly to the dry ingredients, without pre-soaking. Shortcrust pastry is the choice for most recipes; in the past, puff pastry was regarded as a luxury and only affordable by more affluent households.

Introduction

Visitors entering Cornwall, either across Bodmin Moor or over the Tamar Bridge, may not know that they are entering a land of saints and legends, with strong links to Wales and Brittany. Until the mid nineteenth century and the coming of the railways, Cornwall was almost cut off from the rest of England and closer to Brittany by sea.

This is one reason why cooking methods in Cornwall are so different. The connection is not only reflected in the Cornish language but in the cuisine, with dishes such as figgy hobbin, likky pie, kettle broth and, of course, the bright yellow saffron buns.

Cornwall's food traditions stem from being a county of contrasts, from bleak uplands to the flatter landscape near Land's End, an area scattered with numerous ancient monuments. The milder climate of the southern estuaries and harbours, as well as sub-tropical valleys, contrasts with the rougher seas and bracing climate of the North coast. Both the Lizard and Roseland peninsulas have their own distinct characteristics.

At one time most small villages had their own butcher and baker. Now, such local businesses have mostly been replaced by the larger supermarkets. But Cornwall is not just the land of pasties and cream, it boasts a wide variety of different dishes, taking advantage of the surrounding waters and the mild winter climate, often allowing the cattle to graze outdoors on the rich grasslands all the year round. Much has changed over the years, but the recipes survive, as this collection shows.

As a resident of Cornwall, I have enjoyed researching, cooking and sampling these recipes and I hope that you will too.

Carolyn Martin

Soups

Kettle or kiddly broth

An economical soup from the cottage kitchen. A kettle is a large domed cover which was usually used to cover the bread as it bakes in the cloam oven, set inside the fire. The ingredients for the soup can vary depending on what is to hand, in the garden or larder.

Ingredients
> 2 large onions
> 1 leek
> 1 litre (1 3/4 pints) beef stock
> 300 ml (1/2 pint) milk
> 25g (1 oz) butter or margarine
> seasonings according to taste
> slices of white or brown bread, cut into triangles

Method
Melt the butter gently in a large saucepan, before adding the peeled and chopped vegetables. Braise slowly for about 15 minutes, then add the beef stock and other seasonings. Simmer for 30 minutes, until the vegetables are cooked and soft. The soup can be liquidized at this stage although it was traditional to keep the vegetables whole. Add the milk to the soup and warm through before pouring over the slices of bread placed in individual soup bowls. Marigold petals or any other edible flowers can be scattered over the surface, to give colour and interest.

An even simpler version of Kettle broth is to use:

> 2 large onions – left whole
> knob of butter
> 1-2 rounds of bread
> salt and pepper

Method
Cover the onions with water and boil until tender. Remove the onions from the stock, add a knob of butter to the remaining stock, with salt and pepper to taste. Cut the bread into squares and put into individual soup bowls. Pour the soup over the bread and eat while hot.

Swede and saffron soup

It is thought that saffron was introduced into Cornwall by the Phoenicians, trading in tin, long before the rest of England. Saffron is the most expensive of all spices and is usually used in baking. This is an everyday soup from the far west of Cornwall and enhanced by the addition of Cornish cream.

Ingredients
>   50g (2 oz) butter
>   225g (8 oz) swede (peeled and chopped)
>   110g (4 oz) leeks (chopped)
>   1 large onion (sliced)
>   2 sticks of celery (chopped)
>   1 litre (1 3/4 pints) chicken stock
>   1 bay leaf
>   1 tbsp parsley (chopped)
>   1/2 tsp dried mixed herbs
>   6 saffron threads, soaked overnight in a little water
>   110 ml (4 fl oz) Cornish double cream
>   salt and pepper to taste

Method
Melt the butter in a pan and add the prepared vegetables. Cook gently over a low heat for about 10 minutes before adding the stock, bay leaf, parsley and mixed herbs. Simmer for about 30 minutes and once the vegetables are cooked, remove the bay leaf and liquidize. The soaked saffron threads and water are added at this stage. Finally, add the cream and seasonings to taste.

Crab soup

With an abundance of seafood in Cornish waters, crab soup used to be cooked quite regularly. This recipe is for a creamy, rich soup and is almost a complete meal.

Ingredients
>   225g (8 oz) crab meat, half brown and half white
>   1 large onion (peeled and cut in half)
>   1 clove of garlic (crushed)
>   1.2 litres (2 pints) fish stock

50g (2 oz) butter or margarine
25g (1 oz) plain flour
150ml (1/4 pint) double cream
1 tbsp sherry

Method

Melt the butter (or margarine) over a medium heat before adding the onion and garlic. Cover and soften, without allowing the onion to colour, then add the brown crab meat. Stir well and add the flour, stir again to prevent lumps forming before adding the fish stock and bring to the boil. Simmer gently for 30 minutes then remove and discard the onion. Season the remaining stock to taste. Add the cream, sherry and white crab meat and warm through. Serve at once with a slice of home-made bread.

Flat poll or cream of cabbage soup

Cabbage is one of our oldest vegetables and flat poll cabbage used to be grown in abundance in Cornwall as fodder for cattle but it has fallen into disuse. It is now regarded as a heritage variety. Savoy or other hard cabbage can be used in this recipe.

Ingredients

1/4 Savoy or other hard cabbage (shredded)
110g (4 oz) cooked chicken or pork
2 slices of streaky bacon
1.2 litres (2 pints) chicken or ham stock
1 onion (peeled and sliced)
salt and pepper to taste
1 tsp sugar
1 sprig of rosemary, 2 bay leaves and 1 tsp mixed herbs
150ml (1/4 pt) single cream

Method

Slice the meat and add to the stock together with the onion and cabbage, rosemary, bay leaves, mixed herbs. Sweeten with 1 tsp sugar before adding salt and pepper, to taste. Simmer gently for 1 1/2 hours until you have a thick broth. Check the seasoning and finish with the cream.

Parsnip and asparagus soup, a recipe from the Roseland

Both parsnips and asparagus grow well in Cornwall and this soup is deliciously rich, with egg yolks and cream. There is quite a difference between the recipes used in the humble cottage kitchen and those cooked in some of Cornwall's more affluent households. This is a soup that could have been served to grace the table of any of Cornwall's stately homes.

Ingredients
    450g (1lb) peeled parsnips
    225g (8 oz) asparagus
    25g (1 oz) butter
    2 tbsp single cream
    4 tbsp natural yogurt
    $1/4$ tsp ground nutmeg
    2 egg yolks
    salt and pepper to taste

Method
Chop the parsnips and cook in salted water with the asparagus for about 15 minutes or until tender. Once cooked, cut off the asparagus tips and put on one side. Keep the rest of the cooking liquid then blend and puree the remaining vegetables. Melt 25g (1 oz) butter in 1.2 litres (2 pints) of the cooking liquid before adding the pureed vegetables. Heat again and add the ground nutmeg, yogurt and cream. Separately whisk the egg yolks with a little of the warm liquid and pour into the soup. Heat through again, season to taste and dilute with more stock if necessary. The asparagus tips should be scattered over the soup just before serving.

Pea soup, a recipe from North Cornwall

Ingredients
    225g (8 oz) dried peas
    1 bay leaf
    sprig of both thyme and mint
    1 carrot, peeled and sliced
    1 onion (chopped)
    1 rasher of bacon, (chopped)
    1 leek (sliced)

420 ml (³/4 pint) milk
salt and pepper to taste
chopped mint
50g (2 oz) clotted cream
croutons (optional)

Method

Soak the dried peas in cold water overnight. The next morning, add 900 ml (1¹/2 pints) of water to the drained peas. Add the remaining ingredients apart from the milk and seasonings and simmer for 2 hours. Remove the bay leaf and once soft liquidize and add the milk and seasonings. Heat through and serve with a garnish of chopped mint, decorating each bowl with a generous spoonful of clotted cream and croutons (optional)

Savouries and starters

Buttered crab

Ingredients

110g (4 oz) crab meat, a mixture of brown and white
2 anchovy fillets (mashed)
1 cup breadcrumbs
1 glass white wine
3 tbsp butter (melted)
¹/4 tsp nutmeg
salt and pepper to taste

Method

Combine the mashed anchovy fillets with the breadcrumbs and nut-meg. Add the wine and seasonings and simmer gently for 5 minutes. Mix the crab meat with the melted butter and add this to the wine mixture and simmer again for 5 minutes. Serve with fingers of hot buttered toast together with a side salad.

Bread sops – a between meals 'filler'

Cut slices of bread from a crusty loaf (rather than sliced bread). Cut again into small pieces and place in a cup. Pour boiling water over the bread, drain and squeeze with the back of a spoon until the bread is dry and crumbly. Add salt and pepper to taste with a good knob of butter.

Cream and anchovy savoury

An attractive starter, dark anchovies contrasting with the clotted cream.

Ingredients
    4 slices of white bread
    small tin of anchovy fillets – about 30g (1 1/4 oz)
    50g (2 oz) butter
    4 tbsp clotted cream

Method
Cut the bread into squares, roughly 5 cm (2 inches) square. Melt the butter in a large frying pan and fry the bread until golden. Once cooked, place well drained anchovies on each square of fried bread and top with a spoonful of Cornish clotted cream.

Baked rice omelette

A Cornish twist on a recipe for a well known omelette.

Ingredients
    175g (6 oz) long grain rice
    6 free range eggs (beaten)
    1 tsp parsley (chopped)
    salt and pepper, to taste

Method
Boil the rice in 600 ml (1 pint) of water and cook until the rice has been absorbed into the water. Leave the rice to cool and then add the beaten eggs, chopped parsley and seasoning. Turn into a greased ovenproof casserole and bake at 190°C/375°F/Gas 5 for approximately 20 minutes, until the surface turns an attractive golden brown.

The resulting omelette can be varied with the addition of the usual omelette ingredients, such as ham, cheese or mushrooms.

Cheese

With all the rich creamy milk in Cornwall, there were many small cheese makers in the county prior to WW2 . Government restrictions forced many to close but more recently there has been an upsurge in artisan cheese making in Cornwall. Yarg, a cheese with garlic and wrapped in nettles, is probably the best known but there is a Cornish Gouda, a Cornish Blue and Cornish Brie, Davidstow Cheddar as well as the milder hard cheeses, Menallack amongst others.

Fish

With most of Cornwall surrounded by sea, fish was very much on the menu in the past. Mackerel and pilchards were caught in abundance and made a cheap and nutritious meal. These large shoals of fish disappeared from the scene in the late 19th century and are no longer so plentiful.

Travelling to Cornwall in 1810, Joseph Farrington (1747-1821), landscape painter and diarist, observed that the fishermen and their families lived on fish, bread and potatoes.

Herring hot pot

A 'hotpot' usually refers to Lancashire hotpot, with lamb or mutton chops layered with potatoes and cooked slowly in a covered casserole. The Cornish though have their own hot pot (two words) with herrings.

Ingredients
- 4 herrings or mackerel
- 3 spring onions, sliced
- 1 small turnip (or swede), peeled and sliced
- 4 tomatoes, chopped
- 1 tbsp chopped parsley
- 1 bay leaf
- small knob of dripping
- salt and cayenne pepper according taste

Method
Melt the dripping in a small pan and add the sliced spring onions, the chopped tomatoes and sliced turnip. Add the bay leaf and cook for 10 minutes in a covered pan. While the vegetables are cooking, prepare the fish by removing the heads and tails, split open and then fillet, removing the backbone and as many of the smaller bones as possible. Most fishmongers will do this for you. Roll up the fish and tie with cotton before placing the herrings in the pan over the cooked vegetables. Add a little stock, salt and cayenne pepper and cook gently for around 20 minutes or until all the vegetables are soft. Remove the cotton from the fish, scatter with parsley, before serving with mashed potatoes, the vegetables and freshly made mustard.

Baked stuffed bream

Ingredients
>1 bream per person
>suet and seasoned breadcrumbs, in equal proportions,
>>depending on the size and number of bream used
>1 tbsp parsley (chopped)
>butter to dot over the fish before baking

Method
You can clean the fish yourself by scraping off the coarse scales and removing the smaller bones or you can ask the fishmonger to do this for you. To make the stuffing, combine the suet and seasoned breadcrumbs and add the chopped parsley. Moisten and use to stuff inside the fish. Dot the bream with butter before placing in a baking dish. Cook for around 30 minutes, depending on the size of the fish. Oven 180°C/350°F/Gas 4.

Stargazy pie

No Cornish cookery book should fail to mention Stargazy Pie, served in the Ship Inn Mousehole on 23 December, Tom Bawcock's Eve. Tom Bawcock is remembered because, according to the 16th century legend, he saved the villagers from starvation when he ventured out to sea on a particularly stormy night, returning with a full catch and sufficient fish to feed the whole village. The fish were then baked in a large pie, with their heads sticking out of the pastry to show that the pie did indeed contain fish. Since the 1950s the date has been marked by a parade in the village with the pie and this is then served in the Ship Inn, with donations to charity.

Originally pilchards were the only fish in the pie but as they became more scarce, mackerel and herrings were added, as well as rashers of bacon and hard boiled eggs. The Ship Inn tends to omit the bacon and eggs today, aware that some customers may have allergies and would prefer to avoid such food items, but they include white fish, depending on what is available in the fish market that day.

Ingredients
>225g (8 oz) shortcrust pastry, made with plain flour
>8 pilchards, sardines or small herrings
>salt and pepper

1 large onion (chopped)
3 tbsp chopped parsley
3 hard boiled eggs (chopped)
3 rashers of streaky bacon (chopped)
beaten egg to glaze

Method

Roll out the pastry to line a pie plate, brushing the edges with water. Roll another piece for the lid but keep this on one side.

Clean and fillet the fish, leaving the heads in place. Season the insides and stuff with the chopped onion and parsley. Fold over and place on the pie plate with the fish heads on the rim, filling the gaps between the fish with chopped bacon and hard boiled eggs. Cover with pastry, allowing the fish heads to poke through. Alternatively, the heads can be removed when the fish are filleted and cleaned and these are then pushed into the pastry before baking. Brush with beaten egg and bake in a hot oven 200°C/400°F/Gas 6 for 30 minutes. If the fish are large a longer cooking time should be allowed, reducing the temperature to 180°C/350°F/Gas 4 for an extra 15 minutes. Serve hot from the oven.

Cod Kernewek

Apples and cheese covering the fish give an unusual sweet/sour flavour.

Ingredients

4 small cod steaks – other white fish fillets can be used
    just as successfully
lemon juice
salt and pepper
2 cooking apples, such as Bramley, grated
30g (1 1/2 oz) Cheddar cheese (grated)
2 tbsp breadcrumbs and a few knobs of butter

Method

Lay the cod steaks or fillets in a buttered oven-proof casserole and sprinkle the fish with lemon juice, salt and pepper, according to taste. Cover the cod with grated apple, followed by the grated Cheddar cheese. Scatter the breadcrumbs over the fish, dot with butter before adding about 2 tbsp water to the casserole and baking in a 'brisk' oven 200°C/400°F/Gas 6 for about 20 minutes or until nicely browned.

Marinated herrings, pilchards or mackerel

Salting was a useful way to preserve herrings or pilchards in the past but the high price of salt put this out of reach for many families. Marinating herrings is another useful method to preserve fish. The following recipe is based on the ingredients suggested in a recipe book dated 1692, from the Pendarves estate in Cornwall.

Ingredients
>   4 herrings
>   1 tsp salt and 1 tsp black pepper
>   1/4 tsp cochineal
>   1/2 tsp powdered cloves
>   1/4 tsp powdered nutmeg
>   1 bay leaf per fish
>   300ml (1/2 pint) red wine
>   150ml (1/4 pint) cold tea
>   150ml (1/4 pint) malt vinegar

Method
Prepare the fish by washing and cleaning and cut off the heads and tails. Remove the main bones but there is no need to take out all the bones because these are softened with the long, slow cooking process. Rub the salt, pepper, cochineal and the other spices into the fish, placing a bay leaf in each. Roll up to a roll-mop shape and place in an oven-proof casserole. Pour the red wine, cold tea and vinegar over the fish and cover (traditionally the casserole would be covered with brown paper) and bake in a slow oven 150°C/300°F/Gas 2 for 2 1/2-3 hours. Leave until quite cold before removing the fish, now tinged pink from the cochineal and red wine. Serve to accompany a crisp summer salad.

Smoked mackerel custard (for two people)

Smoking is another way of preserving fish and it also gives it a special flavour. An egg custard is usually served as a desert but here it is cooked with smoked mackerel as a savoury, resulting in a surprisingly tasty main course meal.

Ingredients
>   1 fillet of smoked mackerel (flaked, with the dark skin removed)

2 sticks of celery (chopped)
25g (1oz) closed cup mushrooms (sliced)
2 eggs
300ml ($^1/_2$ pint) milk
3 tsp cornflour
2 tbsp double cream
2 tbsp parsley (chopped)
salt and paprika or cayenne pepper, to taste
butter for greasing

Method

Generously butter an oven-proof casserole and add the flaked mackerel, mushrooms and celery. Beat the eggs and blend the cornflour with a little milk before combining with the eggs and the rest of the milk. Add salt and cayenne or paprika pepper to taste followed by the chopped parsley, and double cream. Pour over the fish and bake in a moderate oven, 160ºC/325ºF/Gas 3 for 40 minutes or until the custard is set.

Serve with lightly grilled mashed potatoes and a green vegetable.

Dippie

When cream was readily available in the farm kitchen, dippie was regarded as a treat by many families. It was quick and easy to prepare: potatoes and pilchards were boiled together in thin cream and the dish was eaten while hot.

Vegetables

Potatoes and other vegetables were once the mainstays of the Cornish diet. In his book *A Cornish Childhood*, the historian A L Rowse (1903-1997) writes about his grandmother's ingenuity in feeding her family on a limited budget. There was 'teddy' and turnip pie and sometimes potato and turnip stew: teddy was the local word for potato. Turnips were grown for both the family and livestock

Swedes with bacon

Layer slices of smoked bacon and thinly sliced swedes (or turnips) in a saucepan. Add 2 tbsp of cold water and place on a low heat. Cook until the swedes are cooked and soft. Eat while hot.

Potato cake

Ingredients
- 225g (8 oz) cooked potatoes, mashed
- 110g (4 oz) butter or dripping
- 110g (4 oz) chopped bacon, lightly cooked
- plain flour
- 1 tsp baking powder
- salt and pepper to taste

Method

Rub the butter or dripping into the mashed potatoes and add sufficient flour to bind the mixture together. Add the bacon and baking powder and season to taste. Roll out on a floured surface, shaping into a round to about 2.5 cm (1 inch) thick, at the same time. Bake on a greased baking sheet for 30 minutes at 200°C/400°F/ Gas 6

Serve hot from the oven, spreading with Cornish butter if feeling indulgent but it is delicious left plain.

Likky pie

Likky is the name for leeks in Cornwall.

Ingredients
- 4 leeks
- 2 rashers of unsmoked back bacon
- 1 egg
- 150ml (1/4 pint) cream (or 150ml milk with 1 tbsp butter)
- 175g (6 oz) suet crust pastry

Method

Wash the leeks well and cut into 2.5 cm (1 inch) pieces. Cover with boiling water and infuse for 10 minutes, then drain. Meanwhile cut the bacon into thin slices and layer the bacon with the leeks in a 600ml (1 pint) pie dish, until the dish is full. Season to taste with salt and pepper and cover with suet crust pastry. Bake at 190°C/375°F/Gas 5 for 20 minutes then remove the pie from the oven. Carefully lift the pastry lid and pour the cream and egg over the leeks and bacon. Replace the lid and return to the oven and bake for a further 10 minutes. Serve hot with vegetables and a light gravy.

Chipple pie

Chipple pie is similar to Licky pie. Chipple refers to shallots and shortcrust pastry is used instead of suet crust.

Ingredients
Note – the quantities of chipples and bacon depend on the size of the tart tin, this recipe is for a 20 cm/8 inch tin.

225g (8 oz) shortcrust pastry
chipples, chopped
streaky bacon, diced
2 eggs
salt and pepper to taste

Method
Line a tart tin with shortcrust pastry and fill with chipples and streaky bacon. The bacon should fill the gaps between the chipples. Beat two eggs together and pour over the chipples before covering with a pastry lid. Prick the pastry with a fork and bake at 175°C/350°F/Gas 4 for 45 minutes.

Many cooked vegetables benefit from a touch of clotted cream. Mashed swedes (or turnips) given a dash of pepper and a spoonful of clotted cream will tempt any reluctant turnip eater. Warm spinach and runner beans can be paired with clotted cream and for a special occasion, try filling jacket potatoes with clotted cream and chopped chives.

Pies and pasties

It is said that when the devil crossed the Tamar and heard that Cornishwomen put anything at all in their pies and pasties, he turned tail and quickly headed back to the safety of Devon. No wonder, some of the old cookery books give recipes for pies and pasty fillings with ingredients that are not allowed today, such as larks, rooks, or curlews.

Other pies and pasties in the past included conger pie, giblet pie, muggety pie, herby pasty, date pasty and even mackerel pasty, although it was thought bad luck to take a pasty out to sea. There is even a Windy Pasty when a basic pasty case is baked without a filling and around five minutes before the final cooking time, it is filled with jam and returned to the oven for the remaining time. The dictionary describes a pasty as a pie without a dish and Lancashire pasties are said to be made with less pastry but with more meat. Pasties on sale today can be either savoury or sweet, sometimes a mixture of both.

Pasties were a convenient lunch for the mine workers especially during the tin mining boom of the 19th century and were often marked with the owner's initial, so that the miner could save his pasty to be eaten later. The pastry had to be strong, usually with shortcrust pastry, because sometimes they were thrown down the mine shaft before lunch time. This snack eaten away from home was called crib in mid-Cornwall, croust in West Cornwall or the drinkings in North Cornwall. Cold tea was the favourite accompanying drink. With the decline in tin mining and miners finding work abroad, the pasty recipe went with them and there are still pasty festivals in Mexico and Australia. Nowadays they are usually eaten hot from the oven, with the pasty held in a paper bag.

Traditional Cornish pasty

Ingredients for 2-3 pasties
   shortcrust pastry
   225g (8 oz) plain flour,
   50g (2 oz) lard
   50g (2 oz) hard margarine
   pinch of salt
   water – approximately 110ml (4 fl oz)

   Filling
   110g (4 oz) (approximately) chuck steak
   1 potato
   1 small swede
   1 onion
   salt and pepper

Method
Rub the fats into the flour and add sufficient water to mix into a workable pastry. Refrigerate while the other ingredients are prepared. The meat should be cut up finely and the onion, potato and the swede peeled and sliced.

Roll out the pastry, about 0.5 cm (1/4 inch) thick, to the desired size using a plate or pan lid to cut into a circular shape. Salt and pepper the pastry and add the finely sliced vegetables and finally the meat over half the circle. Sprinkle with more salt and pepper and dust with flour before folding over into a half moon pasty shape, crimping the edges together.

Crimping is done by pinching the pastry together with the left hand and folding over with the right hand to form a rope like effect on the side of the pasty. There is no need to make a hole in the pastry but brush with milk to give a golden colour. Bake at 200°C/400°F/Gas 6 for ³/₄ hour (with fan ovens 180°C/350°F/Gas 4) then turn down the oven to 120°C/250°F/Gas ¹/₂ for 15 minutes.

Guldize pasty

A different type of pasty was baked by the farmer's wife for the harvesters at Guldize, the Cornish Harvest Festival, celebrated around the time of the autumn equinox. Suet crust pastry was used for the pasty and apples were the usual filling. A larger pie, fitchet or fidget pie, was also baked for the reapers, with bacon, onions and desert apples. There was much feasting around the occasion. Guldize Pudding was a rich steamed pudding similar to Christmas Pudding. One recipe suggests using much stale bread, 2.7 kg (6 lb) flour and 30-40 eggs, so not a pudding to be cooked every day.

Guldize apple pasty

Ingredients
   Suet crust pastry made with 225g (8 oz) plain flour
      and 110g (4 oz) suet with water to mix
   225-350g (8-12 oz) cooking apples, Bramley or similar,
      peeled and chopped
   sugar, according to taste
   milk or beaten egg to brush the pasty before baking

Method
Roll out the pastry and cut into rounds of the desired size. Fill the rounds with sufficient chopped apples to cover half the suet pastry and sprinkle with sugar. Dampen the edges and fold over into a pasty half moon shape and crimp in the usual way. Brush with beaten egg or milk before baking at 200°C/400°F/Gas 6 for 25 minutes. Serve while still warm.

Meat and Poultry

Raw fry (1)

A favourite for cold winter days, especially after Christmas when bacon from the Christmas pig was plentiful. The term 'raw fry' describes the potatoes because even after cooking, they remain white as if raw.

Ingredients – for two people
>   3 large potatoes
>   4 rashers of smoked bacon
>   25g (1 oz) dripping
>   salt/pepper
>   1 tsp cornflour mixed with a little stock
>   vinegar (optional)

Method
Peel potatoes and slice thinly; cut bacon into large pieces. Heat dripping and fry the bacon until sealed and then remove. Put potatoes into the same pan and sear in the hot fat and bacon juices. Add bacon and salt/pepper. Cover and cook on a low heat until the potatoes are just starting to break up. Mix the cornflour with a little stock to thicken and add to the potatoes and bacon. Serve hot with bread and butter, adding vinegar according to taste.

Raw fry (2)

As with Cornish under roast, (see below), the exact ingredients have changed over the years. This recipe is just one version.

Ingredients
>   225g (8 oz) lamb's liver
>   little bacon fat or dripping
>   2 potatoes, peeled and sliced thinly
>   1 onion, peeled and sliced
>   beef stock
>   seasoning to taste

Method
Slice the liver thinly and dip into seasoned flour before frying in the dripping until cooked. Remove from the pan and keep warm. Pour a

little stock into the frying pan and add the chopped onion and sliced potatoes. Cover the pan with a lid and cook gently for around 20 minutes, or until the vegetables are cooked. Serve with the cooked liver and gravy from the vegetables. Extra beef stock can be added, according to taste. A green vegetable to accompany is suggested.

Cornish under-roast

The name Cornish under-roast is deceptive because it is not quite the same as the roast meat usually served as part of a Sunday lunch or dinner. The dish resembles a hotpot with the meat being cooked in a casserole under the potatoes. Various versions of the recipe have evolved over the years, from just steak, onion and potatoes to the inclusion of a wider range of vegetables.

Ingredients
    450g (1 lb) beef steak, rump or similar (in one piece)
    900g (2 lb) potatoes
    2 carrots
    2 onions
    1 small swede
    300 ml (10 fl oz/^{1}/$_2$ pint) beef stock
    salt and pepper

Method
Peel the carrots, onions and swede, cut into small pieces and put in a roasting tin. Melt a small amount of bacon fat in a frying pan and after rolling the steak in seasoned flour, fry lightly to brown and lay on top of the vegetables. Peel the potatoes and cut into thin slices before placing around and on top of the meat. Pour the beef stock over the meat, potatoes and vegetables and cook for 30 minutes at 190°C/375°F/Gas 5.

Reduce the heat to 175°C/350°F/Gas 4 for a further hour, covering the casserole with foil if browning too quickly and adding more stock if necessary. Serve with a green vegetable to contrast with the root vegetables.

Optional: a ring of suet pastry around the edge of the casserole can be added and cooked for the last hour.

Roast goose

Until the Victorians introduced turkey as the chosen bird for Christmas dinner, goose was the usual choice. The geese were often home-reared on Cornish farms and were widely available. As with duck, the traditional accompaniments of sage and onion stuffing, apple sauce, potatoes and green peas were offered, as well as a preference in Cornwall for glazed turnips, cooked in butter and brown sugar.

Much dripping is collected during the cooking process and so it is unnecessary to add extra fat, although in the West Country cider is often poured around the bird and basted as it roasts. The stuffing makes use of rum, a reminder of the days when smuggling was just a way of life and rum was hidden away in the store cupboard.

Ingredients
    4.5 kg (10 lb) goose
    600 ml (1 pint) dry cider
    salt and pepper

Method
Pierce the skin with a sharp knife and pour boiling water over the bird, to crisp the skin. Dry the skin, rub salt and pepper over the goose and fill with the chosen stuffing. There is no need to add extra fat because a good quantity of dripping is collected as the goose roasts. Cider can be added though, pouring 600 ml (1 pint) into the roasting tin and using it to baste the goose as it cooks. Roast at 220°C/425°F/ Gas 7 for 30 minutes and then reduce the temperature to 180°C/350°F/ Gas 4 for approximately 2 1/2 hours. Allow to stand for 30 minutes before carving. One old Cornish cookery book suggests a ladleful of rum should be poured over the Christmas goose and set alight as it is carried to the table.

Apple and rum stuffing

Ingredients
    4 eating apples, cored and sliced
    150ml (1/4 pint) dark rum
    110g (4 oz) fresh breadcrumbs
    1 onion (chopped)
    goose liver, sliced

few leaves of fresh sage
$1/2$ tsp grated nutmeg
salt and pepper

Method
Soak the apples in the rum, overnight. The next day add the bread-crumbs and remaining ingredients. Mix well and use to stuff the goose before roasting.

Poor man's goose

Instead of the traditional roast goose, poor man's goose is a surprisingly tasty and of course much more economical alternative.

Ingredients
225g (8 oz) ox or pig's liver
450g (1 lb) potatoes
1 onion
$1/4$ tsp sage
flour
salt and pepper

Method
Slice the liver and dip into flour before placing on the base of a large pie dish. Parboil the onion with the sage and pour over the liver, adding sufficient water to come half way up the dish. Slice the potatoes and place over the liver, forming a crust. Bake for an hour at 180°C/350°F/Gas 4.

Cornish beef stew

A Cornish beef stew is cooked without the usual braising of the meat.

Ingredients
450-675g (1-1$1/2$ lb) shin of beef
1 onion (sliced)
1 tbsp brown sugar
$1/4$ tsp grated nutmeg
1 tbsp vinegar
450ml ($3/4$ pint) beef stock
salt and pepper

Method

Cut the beef into bite-sized pieces, add the sliced onion and put both into a large ovenproof casserole. Sprinkle with grated nutmeg, salt and pepper and add the remaining ingredients – beef stock, brown sugar and vinegar. Bring to the boil and cook on a low heat in the oven, 150°C/300°F/Gas 2, for an hour and then reduce the heat to 140°C/275°F/Gas 1 for a further 1 1/2 hours. Alternatively, the stew can be cooked on a low heat on the hob for 2 1/2 hours. More stock can be added during cooking process, if necessary.

Serve with root and green vegetables as well as potatoes.

Squab pie

Squab pie can refer to pigeon pie or a pie baked with mutton or lamb, onions and apples. This Cornish recipe is found across the West Country.

Ingredients

450g (1 lb) lean lamb, cubed
2 onions, peeled and chopped
1 tbsp. brown sugar
150 ml (1/4 pint) of lamb stock
2 cooking apples, peeled, cored and sliced
1/4 tsp mixed spice or allspice
salt and pepper
225g (8 oz) shortcrust pastry

Method

Layer the cubed lamb, onions and apples in a 600 ml (1 pint) pie dish. Sprinkle with the mixed spice or allspice, salt and pepper and 1 tbsp brown sugar. Moisten the whole with the stock before covering with shortcrust pastry. Glaze with milk and make cuts in the pastry before baking at 180°C/350°F/Gas 4 for 10 minutes. Lower the temperature to 170°C/325°F/Gas 3 for 1 hour 50 minutes.

Chicken caudle pie

Caudle refers to the egg and cream poured into the pie towards the end of the cooking time, as with Licky Pie. The soured cream in this recipe gives the chicken a distinct flavour and puff pastry adds a special lightness.

Ingredients

450g (1lb) chicken, boned thighs or legs or chicken breast
50g (2 oz) butter
1 onion, skinned and chopped
225g (8 oz) puff pastry
25g (1 oz) parsley, chopped
4 spring onions, trimmed and chopped
salt and pepper
150ml (¼ pint) milk
150ml (¼ pint) soured cream
150ml (¼ pint) double cream
1 egg, beaten, plus extra egg for glazing

Method

Heat the butter in a pan and once melted add the onion, cooking until soft but without browning. Transfer to a 26 cm (10 inch) pie dish. Add the chicken to the pan to brown, then transfer to the pie dish, with the onion. Put the parsley, spring onions, soured cream and milk into the pan and gently bring to the boil. Simmer for a few minutes before pouring over the chicken and onion in the pie dish. Cover with foil and bake for 30 minutes at 180°C/350°F/Gas 5 then leave to cool.

Meanwhile cut the pastry to a size just larger than the pie dish. Cut a narrow strip of pastry from the edge and place this around the rim of the dish, wetting the surface. Once the filling has cooled, place the pastry lid on top of the chicken, making a small hole in the lid. Beat the double cream and eggs together, and brush a little of this over the pastry. Bake for 20 minutes at 200°C/400°F/Gas 6 until the pastry is golden, then reduce the temperature to 180°C/ 350°F/ Gas 4. Pour the cream and egg mixture into the pastry hole, (or you can lift the pastry lid and add in this way) shaking the dish to distribute the egg and cream. Return to the oven and cook for 15 minutes. Leave to stand for 5 minutes before serving.

Hog's pudding

In the North of England and Scotland, black pudding is sold in both butcher's shops and in the cooked meat sections of supermarkets. In Cornwall, hog's pudding is sold in the same way; similar to a sausage in shape and colour, it is one of the signature foods of Cornwall. As the name suggests, pork is the main ingredient. Lightly fried, as part of breakfast or supper, hog's pudding is a useful addition to any meal. For home use, in this recipe hog's pudding is cooked in a basin rather than as the usual sausage shape.

Ingredients
  450g (1 lb) lean pork, minced
  225g (1/2 lb) breadcrumbs
  1 large egg
  mixed herbs
  salt and pepper

Method
Mix the pork and breadcrumbs and add herbs and seasonings. Beat the egg and moisten the mixture and then mix well. Transfer to a greased pudding basin, cover with greaseproof and foil and steam for 3 hours.

Puddings

Apple recipes

Many of the apple trees grown in Cornwall today have long histories as well as Cornish names – there is Cornish Aromatic, Cornish Pine, Tresillian Seedling or Cornish Gillyflower, to name just a few. Consequently there are many apple recipes with Cornish apples and a selection is given below.

When Celia Fiennes, the 17th century traveller to Cornwall, first tasted apple pie with cream in St Austell, she was delighted and complimented the cook. 'It is an apple pie with custard all on top… and so it is a sort of clouted cream, as we call it, with a little sugar, and so put on top of the apple pie. I was much pleased with my supper.'

Apple spice

A traditional family recipe, passed down over the generations.

Ingredients

  4 large cooking apples, peeled and cored
  225g (8 oz) flour (a mixture of wholemeal and white plain flour)
  110g (4 oz) margarine
  110g (4 oz) demerara sugar
  25g (1 oz) sugar
  4 tsp cinnamon

Method

Grease a large oven-proof casserole. Rub the fat into the flour with just 2 tsp cinnamon, add the brown sugar and press the mixture into the bottom of the casserole.

Slice the apples and arrange over the surface, making sure that they stand upright, like soldiers. Mix the remaining cinnamon with the sugar and sprinkle over the apples, Dot the whole with a few knobs of margarine. Bake at 190ºC/375ºF/Gas 5 for 30 minutes

Serve with cream or custard. Some people like to serve apple spice with evaporated milk.

Apple dicky

A recipe from the cottage kitchen, quick and simple to make with the minimum of ingredients. Best eaten whilst still hot from the oven.

Ingredients

  225g (8 oz) plain flour
  50g (2 oz) lard
  1-2 dessert apples, cored and chopped
  pinch of salt
  water to mix
  milk to brush over the surface before baking

Method

Sift the flour and salt together and rub in the lard. Add the finely chopped apples and mix with sufficient water to give a dry but elastic dough. Roll out to a circle, approximately 22 cm (8 inches) across, brush the surface with milk and bake for 30 minutes, at 190ºC/375ºF/ Gas 5.

Apple hat

Another apple pudding for the family, this time enriched with clotted cream.

Ingredients
225g (8 oz) self raising flour
pinch of salt
125g (4 oz) shredded suet
6-8 tbsp cold water
675g (1 1/2 lb) Bramley cooking apples, peeled, cored and sliced
50g (2 oz) raisins
75g (3 oz) sugar
3 whole cloves
1/4 tsp ground ginger
1/4 tsp ground cinnamon
grated rind and juice of 1 orange
50g (2 oz) butter
1 tbsp clotted cream

Method
Sieve flour with the salt and mix in the suet, adding sufficient water to give a light dough/pastry. Roll out to about 0.6cm (1/4 inch) thick and use two thirds of the pastry to line a well greased 1 litre (1 3/4 pint) pudding basin.

Fill the basin with layers of apples, raisins, sugar and spices. Add the orange juice, with the butter cut into small pieces, then cover with the remaining suet pastry. Cover again with foil, secured with string and steam for 2-2 1/2 hours. Turn out on to a serving plate, remove a small piece of pastry from the top of the pudding and drop in a tbsp of clotted cream. Serve while hot, with more clotted cream or custard.

Apple cobs make use of clotted cream in a similar fashion. Cooking apples are cored and filled with mincemeat and enclosed in suet crust pastry, rather like apple dumplings. When cooked, the top of the pastry is cut open and a tbsp of clotted cream is dropped inside, melting over the hot apple.

Helston pudding, with lemon sauce

Helston pudding is associated with Flora Day which is celebrated each year in Helston, usually on 8th May. The festival marks the end of winter with couples dancing the traditional Flora Day dance as they follow the silver band along the streets of Helston. The pudding was generally served alongside Russian cream.

Ingredients

  50g (2 oz) currants
  50g (2 oz) raisins
  1 tbsp chopped candied peel
  50g (2 oz) sugar
  50g (2 oz) breadcrumbs
  50g (2 oz) flour
  pinch of salt
  2 tbsp ground rice
  2 tbsp grated suet
  $1/2$ tsp mixed spice
  $1/2$ tsp bicarbonate of soda
  6 tbsp milk

Method

Mix all the dry ingredients together and dissolve the bicarbonate of soda in the milk. Mix this liquid into the dry ingredients and when well mixed spoon into a greased pudding basin. Steam for at least 2 hours, turn out and serve with lemon sauce and a scoop of clotted cream.

Lemon Sauce

Boil 170g (6 oz) sugar with 60 ml (2 $1/2$ fl oz) water for 5 minutes then add 2 tsp butter. Stir until dissolved and add 1 tbsp fresh lemon juice.

Russian cream

Why this name, Russian cream, is associated with Cornwall, is a mystery but it has long been considered as one of the traditional desserts of the county.

Ingredients
> 600 ml (1 pint) milk
> 2 eggs (separated and the egg whites whisked into peaks)
> 50g (2oz) sugar
> 15g ($^1/_2$ oz) of powdered gelatine (vegetarian options are available) or 5 sheets of leaf gelatine – sufficient to set 900 ml (1 $^1/_2$ pints) of liquid
> few drops of vanilla essence

Method
Combine the sugar, egg yolks and vanilla essence with the milk and sprinkle the gelatine over the liquid or add 5 sheets of pre-soaked leaf gelatine. Bring to the boil gently – the mixture will separate but this is normal. Cool for a short while and fold in the beaten egg whites. Pour into a mould and leave to set. Often the Russian cream will set in attractive layers.

Note that this recipe contains uncooked eggs.

Honey baked custard, a recipe from St Veep

A Cornish variation of the usual baked egg custard, with the liquid honey surrounding the custard as it emerges from the oven.

Ingredients
> butter for greasing
> 3 tbsp runny honey
> 2 eggs
> 300 ml ($^1/_2$ pint) milk
> $^1/_2$ tsp grated nutmeg

Method
Butter a 1.2 litre (2 pint) pie dish and run 2 tbsp of thin honey round the inside. Beat the eggs into the milk and add a further generous tbsp of honey. Pour into the pie dish and grate nutmeg over the surface. Set the dish in a larger dish of water and bake in a moderate oven at 180ºC/350ºF/Gas 4 for 30-40 minutes Serve hot or cold with cream.

Mona pudding

This recipe comes from Penryn and is well over 100 years old. Here the rhubarb is sandwiched between the layers of sponge, resulting in an attractive and interesting pudding.

Ingredients

    1 small 'bundle' of rhubarb, weighing approximately
        175-200g (6-7 oz)
    1 tbsp demerara sugar
    3 eggs and their weight in plain flour, sugar and butter
    1 tbsp milk
    lemon rind (grated)
    1 heaped tsp of baking powder

Method

Cut the rhubarb into 2.5 cm (1 inch) pieces and soften with 1 tbsp demerara sugar. Meanwhile, cream the butter and sugar together, add the eggs, one at a time, followed by the lemon rind and dry ingredients and lastly the milk. Place a little of this mixture 2.5 cm (1 inch) deep, in an oven-proof pie dish. Cover this layer with the rhubarb, without adding too much juice, then top the rhubarb with another layer of the sponge mixture. Smooth the top with a knife dipped into hot water. Bake in a hot oven 190°C/375°F/Gas 5 for 40- 45 minutes, until set and spongy, testing the pudding with a knife which should come out cleanly. Reduce the oven temperature slightly if the top is browning too quickly. Serve hot or cold with custard or cream with extra rhubarb, according to taste.

Lemon meringue pie

A recipe from Trerice, a former Elizabethan manor house set in quiet Cornish countryside and yet close to bustling Newquay. The property is now in the care of the National Trust. Visitors come to Trerice to see the 16th century manor house and gardens but also to sample their famous lemon meringue pie.

The following recipe is a scaled down version of the original which uses six lemons and six eggs for eight portions:

For the pie
  225g (8 oz) shortcrust pastry, sufficient to line a
     deep 20 cm (8 inch) flan dish
  juice and zest of 3 lemons
  85g (3 oz) caster sugar
  200 ml (7 fl oz) water
  3 egg yolks
  3 tbsp cornflour

For the meringue topping
  3 egg whites – room temperature is best
  110g (4 oz) caster sugar
  50g (2oz) caster sugar

Method

Line the flan dish with shortcrust pastry and prick the base. Bake blind by putting a sheet of greaseproof on the base and securing it with baking beans. Bake for 15 minutes at 180°C/350°F/Gas 5.

Remove from the oven and discard the greaseproof paper and beans and return to the oven for a further five minutes at 150°C/300°F/Gas 2. Leave to cool.

While the pastry is cooling, put the caster sugar, lemon juice and zest into $3/4$ of the water (140 ml/5 fl oz). Heat gently and bring to the boil, then cool. Put the cornflour into the remaining water and stir until well mixed in. Add the egg yolks and liquid cornflour to the cooled liquid in the pan, put back on the heat and stir until thickened. Pour this mixture into the flan case and cool.

For the topping, whisk the egg whites until white and then slowly add 110g (4oz) caster sugar. Continue to whisk until a stiff peak is formed. Remove from the mixer, add the remaining 50g (2 oz) sugar and fold into the meringue, making sure that all the sugar has been mixed in. Using a metal spoon, spread the meringue over the filling and bake at 180°C/350°F/Gas 5 for 30 minutes Leave to cool and then serve and enjoy.

Figgy pudding, also known as Currany 'obbin or Figgy duff

We all like our figgy pudding
With all this good cheer
Good tidings we bring to you and your kin
We wish you a Merry Christmas and a Happy New Year
And we won't go until we get some
And we won't go until we get some
So bring some out here.

A West Country Christmas carol when wealthy parishioners gave Christmas treats to the carollers singing at their door. A slice of figgy pudding was one such treat. Some bakers making the pudding used to charge more for a richer pudding, *'Figgy duff 4d figgier duff 5d'*.

Figgy pudding can be steamed or baked and both recipes are given here. Figgy usually refers to raisins rather than figs but figs are included in this recipe.

Steamed figgy pudding

Ingredients

25g (1 oz) self raising flour
2 dried figs, well chopped
50g (2 oz) fresh breadcrumbs
$1/2$ tbsp sugar
1 egg beaten
50g (2 oz) suet
1 tsp allspice – or mixed spice (cloves, nutmeg,
    cinnamon, black pepper)
110g (4 oz) raisins
grated rind of 1 lemon
1 tbsp sherry
milk to mix

Method

Mix the dry ingredients with the figs and raisins, stir in the beaten egg and grated lemon rind, then the sherry and just sufficient milk to mix into a soft dough. Spoon into a well greased 1200 ml (2 pt) basin, cover with greaseproof paper or foil and steam for $3^1/2$ hours. Turn out and serve hot with cream or custard.

Cream teas

Most visitors to Cornwall enjoy a cream tea at some stage during their visit. Whether you put jam and then cream on your scones or cream first depends on where you are. In Devon it is cream first topped by strawberry jam whereas in Cornwall jam goes on first and the scone is then crowned with clotted cream.

At one time, apparently, there was a glut of jam in North Devon but the Cornish say it is that, in Devon, they want to hide their cream whereas the cream in Cornwall is superior and they are proud of it. Until fairly recently, splits (or tuffs as they are known in East Cornwall) were served with cream teas but this tradition has now been overtaken by scones. Recipes for both splits and scones are given. In Devon, splits are also known as cut rounds or chudleighs.

Variations include 'thunder and lightning' – splits or scones served with treacle and clotted cream. A 'Cornish sandwich' is when a day-old scone is cut, filled with jam and cream and then sandwiched together again.

Sour milk is left to set until a crust is formed over the surface and the whey drained off; the remaining curds can be eaten with sugar, treacle or more cream. This used to be a special favourite with children.

Cornish splits

Ingredients
- 1 tsp dried active baking yeast
- 300 ml (10 fl oz) milk warmed to 45°C
- 1 tsp sugar
- 350g (12 oz) plain flour
- 1/4 tsp salt
- 25g (1 oz) butter, melted and cooled

Method
Sprinkle the dried yeast over to the warm milk, stir in the sugar and leave for about 10 minutes, allowing time for the yeast to activate. Sift the flour and salt together and add the cooled melted butter. Add the yeast mixture to the flour and turn out over a floured board and knead until smooth. Place the dough in an oiled bowl, cover with a tea-cloth and leave to rise in a warm place until doubled in size.

Turn out again on to a freshly floured board and shape into about nine buns. Place the buns on a greased square baking tin or tray, 23 cm (9 inches), cover with a tea-cloth and leave to rise in a warm place for around 15 minutes or until well risen. Bake in a hot oven 200°C/400°F/ Gas 6 for 15-20 minutes until browned. Split open and serve with strawberry jam and Cornish clotted cream.

Scones

There are many different recipes for scones, some with plain flour, cream of tartar and bicarbonate of soda whereas other recipes use self raising flour, as in this recipe.

Ingredients

225g (8 oz) self raising flour
$1/4$ tsp salt
25g (1oz) caster sugar (optional)
25g (1 oz) unsalted butter (diced)
1 tbsp clotted cream
125-150 ml (4-5 fl oz) milk
beaten egg or milk to glaze

Method

Sift flour into a bowl and add salt, sugar, clotted cream and butter. Rub in until the mixture resembles breadcrumbs before mixing in the milk. All the milk may not be necessary but sufficient to give a soft, sticky dough. Knead lightly and turn out on to a floured surface and roll out to approximately 1.2-2 cm ($1/2$-$3/4$ inch) thick. Cut out about 6 scones and place on an ungreased baking sheet. Brush the scones with beaten egg or milk before baking at 220°C/425°F/Gas 7 for 10-15 minutes until well risen and golden.

Buns and biscuits
'Cokernut' buns

An unusual Cornish recipe, from a cookery book dated 1913.

Ingredients
> 3/4 teacup of sugar
> 1 teacup of desiccated coconut
> 1 teacup of ground rice
> 1 teacup of plain flour
> 1 good tsp baking powder
> 50g (2 oz) butter (melted)
> 1 egg
> milk for mixing

Method

Mix all the dry ingredients together and mix in the beaten egg and melted butter with sufficient milk to give a soft dropping mixture. Spoon the mixture into paper cases and bake in a 'slow oven' 160°C/325°F/Gas 3 for 30 minutes, or 40 minutes if a crispy topping is preferred.

Saffron buns

The bright yellow saffron buns, displayed in the shop windows of most bakers in Cornwall are another traditional food of Cornwall. A yeast bun is similar and a larger version, a tea treat or feast bun, used to be served to children on Sunday School outings or special festivals.

Ingredients
> 450g (1 lb) strong plain flour
> 8 saffron threads, dried overnight in a warm place and
>   then crushed
> 75g (3 oz) butter
> pinch of salt
> 75g (3 oz) currants and sultanas
> 50g (2 oz) candied peel
> 40g (1 1/2 oz) sugar
> 12g (1/2 oz) fresh yeast *or*
>   1 sachet of instant dried yeast (7g/1/4 oz)
> 1 tsp sugar to activate yeast
> 200 ml (7 fl oz) tepid milk

Method

Soak the dried saffron in 85 ml (3 fl oz) hot water for about an hour. Sift the flour and salt together and rub in the butter followed by the dried fruit and sugar and mix well. Add a tsp sugar to the tepid milk and stir in the fresh or dried yeast and allow time for the yeast to froth and activate. If using fast action yeast, the yeast can be added directly to the dry ingredients, without pre-soaking. Pour the milk and saffron water into the flour and knead into a soft dough. Cover and leave to rise in a warm place for about an hour until doubled in size.

Knock back the dough again and shape into about 12 buns. Leave to rise again, until doubled in size and bake in a hot oven 200°C/400°F/Gas 6 for 10 minutes.

Yeast buns

Ingredients

450g (1 lb) strong plain flour
50g (2 oz) lard
50g (2 oz) butter
pinch of salt
100g (3-4 oz) caster sugar
150g (4-5 oz) sultanas
250 ml (10 fl oz) water
1 tsp sugar
25g (1 oz) fresh yeast or 2 tsp of dried active yeast

Makes about 12 buns

Method

Sieve the flour and salt into a large bowl. Rub in the butter and lard before stirring in the caster sugar and sultanas. Add the yeast or dried active yeast to the warm water and stir in 1 tsp sugar to activate the yeast. Once the yeast is bubbling, pour the liquid into the flour mix before turning on to a floured board. Knead the dough well to smooth out any cracks and return to an oiled bowl, leaving in a warm place for about an hour, until the dough has doubled in size. Return to the floured board, knead lightly and shape into buns. Once well risen, bake for 20 minutes at 180°C/350°F/Gas 4.

St Keverne Feast buns

Many Cornish villages used to celebrate their feast days each year, the celebrations often lasting all week. St Keverne Feast was always on 18 November and until the beginning of 20th century there was a fair and the children enjoyed a two day break from school. There was usually a hunt, families would meet together for a special roast meal and the St Keverne Feasting Song was sung at the concert on Feast Monday.

The St Keverne Feast bun is made without yeast and is a cross between a scone and a biscuit.

Ingredients
    10 saffron threads, soaked in a little water overnight
    225g (8 oz) plain flour
    pinch of salt
    225g (8 oz) self raising flour
    225g (8 oz) butter
    200g (7 oz) caster sugar
    175g (6oz) mixed dried fruit
    milk and water to mix
    egg and syrup for glaze

Method
Sift the flour with the salt and rub in the butter. Add the other dry ingredients then the milk and soaked saffron, mixing into a dough slightly softer than for pastry. Roll out and cut into rounds, a little thinner than scones. Glaze with egg and sugar syrup, marking each bun with a cross. Bake at 190°C/375°F/Gas 5 for 15-20 minutes.

Callington buns

Similar to Rock buns but Callington buns have a hint of lemon.

Ingredients
    225g (8 oz) self raising flour
    110g (4 oz) cooking margarine
    2 medium or 1 large egg (beaten)
    170g (6 oz) sugar
    25g (1 oz) candied lemon peel
    110g (4 oz) mixed dried fruits

lemon essence or 2 tsp fresh lemon juice
milk to mix and then to brush the buns before baking

Method
Sift the flour and rub in the margarine, then add the eggs. Mix well before adding the remaining ingredients, apart from the milk. Add sufficient milk to give a stiff mixture and place the buns in small heaps on a greased baking tray. Brush with milk and bake in a hot oven, 190°C/375°F/Gas 5 for 15-20 minutes.

Rock buns

A recipe from the former Rock Bakery, in Rock, North Cornwall. Weighing out the mixture into 50g (2 oz) pieces is a good way to ensure that all the Rock buns are of equal size. The generous quantity of baking powder is correct.

Ingredients
225g (8 oz) plain flour
12g (1/2 oz) baking powder
65g (2 1/2 oz) butter
65g (2 1/2 oz) sugar
85g (3 oz) sultanas
1/2 tsp ground nutmeg
1 egg, made up to 150 ml (5 fl oz) with milk

Method
Sift the flour and baking powder together, rub in the butter and add the sugar, nutmeg and sultanas. Mix the beaten egg with the milk and add to the dry ingredients, without making the mixture too wet. Place rough heaps, weighing approximately 50g (2 oz) each, on a greased baking tray. Bake at 200°C/400°F/Gas 6 for 10 minutes, until lightly browned.

Garibaldi biscuits

It may seem strange to include a recipe for Garibaldi biscuits in a Cornish cookery book but when Giuseppe Garibaldi, the Italian general, visited Fowey in 1864, he was treated as a local hero. Some say that he visited this country in order to obtain medical treatment but he also wanted to see his friend, John Whitehead Peard, who had fought with Garibaldi in Italy and who was known as Garibaldi's Englishman. Peard entertained Garibaldi at his home at Penquite, near Fowey.

This recipe is similar to the recipe for Cornish 'sly cakes', where puff pastry is rolled out and scattered with currants. The pastry is then rolled again to allow the currants to peep out 'slyly'.

Ingredients
   50g (2 oz) currants
   35g (1 1/2 oz) butter
   110g (4 oz) self raising flour
   pinch of salt
   25g (1 oz) sugar
   about 25 ml (1 fl oz) milk
   extra milk to brush over and sugar to sprinkle over the
      biscuits before baking

Method
Rub the butter into the flour and salt. Add sugar and sufficient milk, about 25 ml (1 fl oz), to make a workable dough. Roll out thinly into a rectangular shape, keeping the ends and sides as straight as possible. Sprinkle the currants over one half of the pastry, fold over the other half and roll out again, thinly, about 0.6 cm (1/4 inch) thick, again keeping the edges as straight as possible.

Carefully lift the pastry on to a well greased baking sheet before cutting into small oblong biscuits with a sharp knife. Brush with milk and sprinkle with sugar. Bake in a hot oven 200°C/400°F/Gas 6 for about 10 minutes, until golden brown.

Ginger fairings

Home made ginger fairings were generally on offer at the many fairs across the county. Very much associated with Cornwall, the fairings are now made commercially.

Ingredients

110g (4 oz) self raising flour
1 tsp bicarbonate of soda
35g (1¹/₂ oz) sugar
1 tsp ground ginger
50g (2 oz) margarine
2 tbsp golden syrup

Method

Sift the flour, bicarbonate of soda and ginger together. Add the sugar and rub in the margarine, lightly, until crumbly. Add the syrup (it may be necessary to warm the syrup slightly, to help with measuring) and mix to a stiff dough. Roll the mixture into about 16 balls and place on a greased baking tray, flattening each ball slightly with the back of a spoon. Space should be allowed for expansion in the oven.

Bake at 190°C/375°F/Gas 5 for10-15 minutes.

Launceston biscuits

A family recipe handed down over several generations, similar to shortbread and often baked for family gatherings and other such events.

Ingredients

110g (4 oz) butter or baking margarine
110g (4oz) sugar
225g (8 oz) self raising flour
1 egg, beaten

Method

Rub the butter (or margarine) into the flour and add sugar and sufficient beaten egg to bind the mixture. It may not be necessary to use all the egg, otherwise extra flour has to be added. Roll out the dough and cut into biscuit shapes with a 6 cm (2¹/₂ inches) fluted cutter. Bake at 160°C/325°F/Gas 3 for 10-15 minutes until slightly crisp.

Cakes

Heavy cake

From his hut high on the clifftop, the huer used to shout 'hevva', pointing to the shoals of fish coming in, to direct the fishermen. As the fish were caught in the nets, back on shore, the women would make the traditional heavy cake, scoring the surface to represent the fishing nets. Others say that the cake was to reward the women for their part in packing and salting the fish.

Ingredients
    450g (1lb) plain flour
    1^1/$_2$ tsp baking powder
    110g (4 oz) hard margarine
    110g (4 oz) lard
    170g (6 oz) mixed dried fruit
    85g (3 oz) sugar
    1^1/$_2$ tsp nutmeg
    pinch of salt
    100-150 ml (4-5 fl oz) milk
    extra sugar to sprinkle over the cake before baking

Method
Rub margarine and lard into the flour before adding the baking powder, sugar, dried fruit and nutmeg. Add milk and mix with a knife into a soft dough. Press mixture together and roll into an oval shape, approximately 1.2-1.8 cm (^{1}/$_2$-^{3}/$_4$ inch) thick, kneading out the cracks. Extra milk can be added if the mixture is too dry. Score the surface diagonally to represent the fishing nets and sprinkle with sugar.

Bake at 190°C/375°F/Gas 5 for approximately 30 minutes, depending on the thickness of the dough. Best eaten whilst still warm.

Penzance, Launceston and St Ives all have fruit cakes bearing their names. The reasons have been lost in history but all the recipes are rather similar. The St Ives cake uses yeast, a reminder that yeast was used as a raising agent in Cornwall for longer than in other parts of Britain. Similar to the rich Cornish black cake, these cakes resemble well fruited Christmas cakes.

Penzance cake

Although not well known in Penzance today, the recipe for Penzance cake dates from the early 18th century, appearing in *The Country Housewife and Lady's Director, in the Management of a House and the Delights and Profits of a Farm*, a book by Richard Bradley, the first professor of botany at Cambridge University. The recipe is for a substantial family fruit cake, with a good taste of ginger and the currants giving a speckled topping. Serve as a cake for afternoon tea or as a pudding, with custard.

Ingredients

450g (1 lb) plain flour
110g (4 oz) caster sugar
1/2 tsp bicarbonate of soda
110g (4 oz) softened butter
2 tsp ground cinnamon
450g (1 lb) currants
225g (8 oz) crystallised (or stem) ginger, chopped
110g (4 oz) mixed peel, finely chopped
2 beaten eggs
150 ml (5 fl oz) tepid milk

Method

Using a large bowl, sift the flour and add the sugar and bicarbonate of soda then rub in the butter. Add the cinnamon, currants, ginger and peel, followed by the beaten eggs and milk. Mix well and spoon the mixture into a greased and lined 22cm (9 inch) cake tin. Bake at 150°C/300°F/Gas 2 for 1 1/2–1 3/4 hours, until a knitting needle or skewer comes out clean when tested. Turn down the oven towards the end of the cooking time to prevent the cake from browning too quickly and cover with a piece of brown paper. Leave for at least a day before cutting.

A smaller cake can be made with half the quantity, using a 15-18 cm (6-7 inch) square tin, cooking for 1 1/4 -1 1/2 hours but turning down the oven to 130°C/250°F/Gas 1/2 after 45 minutes. Cover with brown paper towards the end of cooking time, to prevent the surface from browning and becoming hard.

Launceston cake

Launceston has always played an important part in Cornish history and was the county town until the early 19th century when this honour moved to Bodmin then Truro. The Launceston cake recipe has been in use for many years, a dark fruit cake and similar to a Christmas cake but not quite as rich. Unlike Penzance cake which includes stemmed ginger, Launceston cake has ground almonds, black treacle and lemon peel.

Ingredients
  225g (8 oz) self raising flour
  50g (2 oz) ground almonds
  170g (6 oz) butter
  170g (6 oz) granulated sugar
  1 tbsp syrup
  1/2 tbsp black treacle
  450g (1 lb) currants
  50g (2 oz) lemon peel (or mixed peel)
  3 eggs

Method
Cream the butter and sugar together before adding the syrup and treacle. Mix in well and add the eggs, one at a time. Sprinkle in the currants and lemon peel, then fold in the flour and ground almonds. Spoon into a greased and lined 20cm (8 inch) cake tin and bake for 1 1/2 – 2 hours at 180°C/350°F/Gas 4. Turn the oven to a lower temperature if browning too much and cover with a piece of brown paper or foil.

Spicy tea cake, from St Austell

There is a similar recipe in Redruth and baked in the same way. It is suggested that you should wait a day before cutting into the tea cake.

Ingredients
  110g (4 oz) cooking margarine
  110g (4 oz) caster sugar
  225g (8 oz) self raising flour
  1 cup of cold tea
  225g (8 oz) mixed dried fruit

1 tsp bicarbonate of soda
1 tsp mixed spice
1 egg

Method

Put the margarine in a large saucepan and add the dried fruit and cold tea. Bring to the boil and simmer for 2 minutes. Leave to cool then add the remaining ingredients, flour, egg, sugar, bicarbonate of soda and mixed spice. Mix well and spoon into a well greased and lined 450g (1 lb) loaf tin. Bake at 180°C/350°F/Gas 4 for 50–60 minutes, check after 50 minutes, and turn down the oven if browning too quickly.

Chirky wheeler

Chirks is an old Cornish dialect word for cinders from the fire. In the past the cake used to be cooked on a pre-heated flat plate on an open fire, hence the name. Nowadays, chirky wheeler is usually cooked on a low heat in a frying pan.

Ingredients

225g (8 oz) plain flour
3/4 tsp baking powder
110g (4 oz) butter or cooking margarine
75g (3 oz) currants
25g (1 oz) sugar (optional)
pinch of salt
milk to mix

Method

Roughly rub the butter or margarine into the flour, salt and baking powder, add the currants and sugar (if used) before adding sufficient milk to mix into a pliable dough. Roll the dough on a floured board, to a size sufficient to fit into a 20 cm (8 inch) wide well-greased frying pan. Cook on the stove on a low heat, turning as necessary until cooked through and slightly browned and burnt at the edges. Serve with clotted cream, ice cream or jam.

Farmhouse cider cake

Quick and easy to make, with the nutmeg and cider giving the cake a pleasing caramel colour. Serve as a cake or as a pudding, with pouring cream.

Ingredients

225g (8 oz) plain flour
1 tsp bicarbonate of soda
2 eggs
3/4 tsp grated nutmeg
110g (4 oz) sugar
110g (4 oz) butter
1 cup cider – 200 ml (7 fl oz) – beaten to a froth

Method

Sieve the flour, nutmeg and bicarbonate of soda together. Cream the butter and sugar then add the eggs. Fold half of the flour into the creamed mixture before pouring in the cider. Add the remainder of the flour and mix well. Bake in a greased and lined 20 cm (8 inch) cake tin in a moderate oven 180°C/350°F/Gas 4 for 45 minutes.

Miscellaneous

Apple spiced ginger

A useful preserve, an acceptable alternative to marmalade on the breakfast table or spread on top of warm homemade scones and topped with Cornish clotted cream.

Ingredients

1.15kg (2 1/2 lb) apples, cooking or desert
0.9 kg (2 lb) sugar
300 ml (1/2 pint water)
1 lemon
65g (2 1/2 oz) stem ginger (chopped)
1 tsp ground ginger

Method

Peel and cut up the apples and place in a large pan with the water. Squeeze and zest the lemon and add the juice and zest to the apples with the ground ginger. Tie the apple peelings and lemon pips into a secure muslin bag and add to the pan. Cook gently until all the apples are soft. Remove the muslin bag before adding the sugar and stem ginger. Boil briskly until setting point is reached – this can be tested by putting a spoonful on a cold saucer and checking to see if the surface of the preserve wrinkles.

Kea plum jam

Kea plum jam is much sought after in Craft Fairs over the summer months, not only for the flavour but also because supplies of the fruit are limited. Kea plums grow best in quite a small area, around Kea, a creekside area near Truro. More like a damson than a Victoria plum and with a tart, rich yet full flavour, Kea plums are rich in pectin and ideal for jam making.

Ingredients
   1.3 kg (3 lb) Kea plums
   juice of 1 lemon
   1.3 kg (3 lb) preserving sugar
   300 ml (1/2 pint) water

Method
Remove the stones from the plums (or you can do this at a later stage by skimming off the stones as they rise to the surface when boiling). Place the Kea plums in a large preserving pan, add the water and lemon juice and boil until the fruit is soft and pulpy. Turn down the heat and add the sugar, then boil rapidly until the setting point is reached. This can be tested by putting a spoonful of jam on a cold saucer. It is ready when pushed with a finger and wrinkles form on surface. Bottle and store or enjoy the jam with scones or splits and with Cornish clotted cream.

Cornish mincemeat

A Christmas recipe from the past when mince pies were shaped into an oblong to represent the manger in the Nativity scene.

Ingredients
> 450g (1 lb) beef suet
> 450g (1 lb) currants
> 450g (1 lb) raisins
> 450g (1 lb) apples (peeled and chopped)
> 2-3 eggs
> 1 tsp allspice
> pinch of salt
> brandy and wine, quantity according to choice

Method
In a large bowl, mix all the ingredients together, beat well and sweeten to taste. Finally add 'as much brandy and wine as you like'.